r

es

for

rs

ch

First published in the UK in 2010 by
Christian Education Publications
1020 Bristol Road
Selly Oak
Birmingham
B29 6LB

British Cataloguing-in-Publication data:
A catalogue record is available for this book from the British Library.

ISBN: 978-1-905893-35-5

Designed and typeset by:
Wordsense Ltd, Edinburgh.

Printed and bound in the UK by:
Cromwell Press Group, Trowbridge, Wiltshire.

Acknowledgements: see back of book.

Contents

introduction 5

beginnings & endings 7

humanness & godness 21

relationship & knowing god 39

love & jesus 57

wisdom & wonder 73

trust & darkness 89

prayer & blessings 107

Acknowledgements 125

Bibliography 126

Index 127

About the author

Jane has been writing since childhood and has won prizes for her poetry. Her writing links a love of this planet, its rocks and oceans and trees and bees, with an exploration of the paths and patterns we and God weave.

She has qualifications in biology, geology and theology and also in counselling, education and pastoral studies. She has studied energy work and endorphins with William Bloom and learnt much from John O'Donohue, Julia Cameron and Mary Oliver.

Her journey with God has included living in community as a member of the Findhorn Foundation, celebrating Jewish festivals with her family and pursuing authentic Christianity. Her writing has roots in the traditions of both Christianity and Holistic spirituality. She is particularly interested in Celtic spirituality and its view of creation as a self-giving of God.

Jane is a commissioned writer for Word Live, a daily on-line bible engagement experience. She is a commissioned minister leading services within a local church and running groups in the community, and she accompanies people on their spiritual journey.

Her life experiences include working with young people, the unemployed, and people with a mental health or substance-abuse problem. She and her husband Bill have two daughters, Joy and Grace. They live on the western edge of London.

www.janeupchurch.co.uk

Introduction

I set out to write this book in response to losing faith in the religious systems that had previously nurtured me. Finding myself on the outside trimmed the fat on my theology. It also gave me a much bigger community, a community where many people had an interest or belief in God or spirituality in some way but often did not want to commit to a tight religious structure. I wrote this for those who feel on the outside of religion to share ways of being on the inside of God, and for those whose faith lies within the form of religion to find expressions of God beyond the boundaries.

This book is about life and God and an everyday spirituality. I have wanted to explore God in a way that anyone can access, in a way that gives room for your thoughts and responses, not just my own. We all live in this world, not in heaven; we all live in our bodies, not as spirits. This is the place, if anywhere, to find wonder and fulfilment, to learn the lessons of love, to appreciate taste and texture and colour, to make our peace with who we are and the places we touch. This is the arena of God.

It is a wonderful freedom to engage with God in the everyday, to live a life where the physical and the spiritual nurture each other and know the patience within both for our fumblings and forgettings. We are not small beings; we hold an ocean of possibilities inside us; we have an interface with God around us. Sometimes the immensity and simplicity of this make it hard to focus. I find help in reading the thoughts of others who walk within both these worlds, and in writing about it myself. So I offer this book with pieces, quotes, questions and thoughts for your reading, and space for your writing or drawing if that's how you like to respond.

Jane Upchurch

'No one has the right to deny you the beautiful adventure of God.'
John O'Donohue

beginnings & endings

Some beginnings were birthed before we drew breath, most seem beyond our control. But each day we hold the power to initiate or create something new with our lives. Where would you like to make a new beginning?
Can you also find creative ways to deal with endings?

Inner wellies

Each morning
I'm going to put on
my inner wellies
so I can splosh and slop
through all the floods and mud
life sends me
instead of tiptoeing round the edge
or getting stuck in the muck.

Daily beginnings. Our life brings the universe into one point, lived day by day.

In the beginning

In the beginning, the black emptiness of space
then light bursting,
a million stars and suns the darkness could
not hide,

infinity and eternity winding through the
heartbeat of God starting to
measure time,

the mind of God imagining, planning and
preparing a myriad forms of life,

the image of God fleshed out as man and
woman, you and me

in three-fold harmony,

in the beginning.

Cosmic beginnings. We are part of the birth of the universe, linked to each other and to God.

Spirit beings

In the beginning
the womb-hidden explosion of life
and urgent, bubbling ball of cells
take shape around lines of energy,
meridians that form a spirit body,
blueprint for physical bodies,
first-formed and always present,
directing our growth.

We are not just flesh and blood,
not just mind, feelings, actions.

We are spirit beings.

Lines of energy
drawn by the finger of God,
spirit bodies
breathed by the breath of God,
spirit to spirit,

present before and after
we are flesh and blood bodies,
singing the music of the stars,
belonging to God.

Can you see yourself as a spirit being?
Can you see your neighbour as a spirit being?

beginnings

I have seen a miracle

I have seen a miracle, the creation of life from part of me and part of you.

I have held a new being in my body when no one could see it, not even I. God's secret.

At 28 days everything was there, heart beating. And the fingers grew without me forming them.

But the biggest miracle was the gift of spirit.

Inside my body was a new person waiting to say 'hello'.

It's easy to see the birth of a baby as a miracle, as a gift from God. But everyone we meet is that same miracle, grown up and walking around. Can you see people as gifts of God?

Glimpsing God

Can I with a heart of clay glimpse God?
Can I with fear and failure as my inner stripe
aspire to more?

Can a numinous, luminous being
mean something to me,
engage me without breaking,
guide me without speaking?

Can my mind grasp the uncontainable,
can my soul have room for such spirit
without losing its own?

Is there a weaver of destiny
who has spotted the dot of my visit in history
and can untangle these threads
without treading on my toes?

Can I find a source for hope?
Can I hold doubt while I believe?
Can I know without understanding,
change without acceding?

Can I trust
that exploring the possibilities of God
will feel like a beginning
and not like an ending?

Can I?

Cross roads

Cross roads,
the challenge and
possibility
of choice
for those who
are free,
God's gift.

Walking one way means leaving another.

Endings and
beginnings
come together
and weave
the pattern
of our lives.
Finding
fulfilment
is always
fingered
by loss,
and loss comes
adorned
with hope.

Endings are easier when we can also see them as beginnings.

For Peggy

(with only a few months to live)

Now is the time to sit in the shelter
of all the happy years
touching again the pleasures, and pains,
and knowing that whatever life brought,
it was good.

Not all have this chance.
A time to reflect
and mend any faults you find.
A place to find peace
like the ripening of a fruit.

And then to see
that the things that matter
are the people in your heart
and the God who holds it.

Find time for laughter as you
look back and count the smiles
or look forward and count the stairs
to heaven.

We can look back and forward at any time. What are the jewels in your path? When you are 80 and look back, what would you want to have done?

Heaven

Heaven
is the suntouch
of God's presence
weighing like motes of gold
the cups of my heart,

a shelter now
that will last the blast
of death.

Some say that fear of death is the root of all fear. Knowing God makes it much easier – God is there already and can help us through.

Autumn leaf

If I were an autumn leaf
would I set red in my hair
to blaze against the dying day

or dust my dress with gold
to light the night
with soft shining?

Would the earth creep into my veins
until I curled and crisped,
an offering for hungry feet,

not to fear the decay of death
but shoot bright a light
to warm hearts on winter's journey?

Endings can be glorious.

For Sammy

Not a sparrow falls
but God knows it,
not a man dies
but God grieves
if in dying they leave
life unfinished,
sour notes not reprieved
and love's thick cords
cut and the wound not healed.

Yet death is not an ending
of hope but an opening door
to where God calls us all.
He alone knows
our heart's deep core
and searches for footprints
of Jesus
to pour love undeserved
in welcome.

Jesus can take away the sting of death.

When I am about to die

endings

When I am about to die
don't cover me in tears or fears
but press close with your love and listen hard
for you will be sure to hear
the steady breath of the One I love
coming to carry me home.

It is a new journey
and I will miss you all, my friends
and sweet parts of my heart,
so bear me up with your blessings.
Don't hold back,
even if I seem asleep my spirit can still hear,
and if this is the last time
I will know your voice this side of heaven
I want to hold it dear
and journey on its waters.

Wash me with your memories of sun
and with your hope,
fill me to the brim
with your tales of our harmonies
and my place in your universe
that I might burst forth from this pod
with the power of your love.

'When your time comes, may you be given every blessing and shelter that you need.'
John O'Donohue, *Anam Cara*

At the end of the day

At the end of the day
when all has gone save the curtained
tomorrow
and I am asked who I am,
what shall I say?

Yesterday there were many words I
might have used
to describe who I am or what I have done
(though what I would most want to be
is someone who has learnt to love,
and to live my life fully).

Today they are gone
and as I look into the arms of eternity
I have one label on my suitcase –
'God's'.

What is your label?

humanness & godness

Spirituality starts with ourselves. How would you describe yourself, the inner bits, the real you? Where, how, why do you experience or need or wonder about God? What kind of God do you picture when you hear the word?
What kind of God do you or don't you believe in?

Three needs

They say we have three needs.

To be loved absolutely, unconditionally;
accepted for who we are not who we
should be.

To love,
for love can't just be taken, it should be
given;
learning to live for others not just for self,
a flowing of heart.

To have a purpose,
to know that without us this world would
not be the same,
to have a goal to attain,
to work and be satisfied, to fill our name.

Three needs and a three-dimensioned God,

God to love, to be loved and to inspire.

Which part of this do you find hardest?

humanness

Only one

There is no one else
who can be you,
who can bring your unique flavour
to the world and the places
where you walk.
You are an indispensable part
of God's mosaic.

'Teach me to search for you in my own depths that I may find you in every living soul.'

J. Philip Newell,
Sounds of the Eternal: A Celtic Psalter

Heart

My heart
is made to live
in God's love and
when I don't
I run
dry.

What would you write in a heart shape?

humanness

Beauty

Beauty
enlarges and inspires
my heart
because it reflects divine beauty
lining my soul.

Have you noticed beauty lining your soul? You could print a photo of yourself to paste here and write 'beautiful' in the middle like a curled cat.

Source of strength

Help doesn't just come
from outside.

There is a hidden place inside
where heart energy
holds life like a fire,
burning any dross that touches it
and replenishing peace.

I have seen this fire a couple of times, seen it burn the swirl of destructive passions like hair in a flame. But I so often live as if it isn't there.

humanness

Blob days

Some days
the sense of God is like magic in each
molecule
shimmering in belly-smiles of joy
and anticipation.

Other days are blob days.
Nothing shimmers and it's hard to decide
whether it's life letting me down
or me letting life down.

Plus various days of in between.

God – blob – God – blob – God.

I guess that pretty much describes us!

I am allowed to make mistakes.

Permission

God gives you permission
to live your own life.

You don't have to live the life of those
you value
or that others say you should.

Yours is enough for you to handle
and the only one you are equipped
to live.

Your life is God's gift to you
and your gift to others.

Enjoy!

**'The glory of God is the human
person fully alive, and the glory of man
is the contemplation of God.'**

Irenaeus, *175 AD*

Community

There is a community of spirit that
engages me
and links my life with others.

We don't live in the same place or worship
with the same group.
We aren't called community.

We create it by recognising the soul-beat of
another searcher,
by sharing and listening to heart.

It doesn't break but stretches across
distances
between people or ideas,
networking inside the mind.

It can go unnoticed as it doesn't control or
dictate,
the threads that link us are invisible.

But without it we would each be less
ourselves,
individuality echoing in a void.

If you are not part of a structured community, whether spiritual or social, have you found ways to relate to others who are on a similar journey?

God

infusing people and place with spirit,
creating and carrying
cells and atoms, stars and worlds
with delight,
holding each being lightly
as only love can,
God being.

Breath of life feeding space and time
with love and honour,
with wisdom and beauty,
patiently unfolding destiny,
God knowing.

Presence of heaven
connecting to bread and wine,
soil and thought,
passionate and positive for life,
hidden yet open
to encounter and adore,
God wooing.

**God is so much more than this,
beyond our words, our space, our time,
yet particular for each person, each
culture. These are some aspects that
are important to me.
What is important to you?**

godness

God participates.

'God is pure verb, a permanent event, an eternal surge, a total quickening.'
John O'Donohue, *Divine Beauty*

I need a God who can suffer

Don't preach to me a God in the sky who only
knows how to smile,
or someone grim who gets angry when I fail.

I need a God on my side,
one who knows how to cry and is willing to
share my pain.

There is too much pain for a heart to hold,
suffering that shatters sense and hurts
innocence.

God, I need you to know my pain,
to throw away the privilege of position that
keeps us apart and come.
I need a God who can suffer.

I need a God who is not above my dirt, who can
sit by me with hurt hands and mend my life
because yours was broken.

I need a God who is willing to walk
everywhere I walk with eyes open.
I need a God who is human.

Could God be human and be God?

Heartbeat

God is the invisible
heartbeat of the
world.

Can you hear its beat?

God changes

God changes
like the tide
like the seasons
like the wind
like the sky.

God changes
when I pray
when I cry.

God changes
like a face
when it smiles.

Some theology says that God never changes (so we can trust that if God is loving yesterday, God will be loving today). But that can seem unresponsive. Do you find it comforting or scary to think of God changing?

godness

God's name

God's name like dirty dollar bills
is handled by everyone for their own
purpose,
base or great

without ever losing value.

**If I insult God it is not God I tarnish,
only myself.**

godness

Outside

The words we use to try and portray God are never sufficient. There is always as much outside as inside our concepts.

'Beyond you there is only more of you, within you there is still the fullness of you.'

Gary Collins, *Sacred Space Ritual*

Yes

If you could sum up God
in one word
would it be
'No',
making rules to oppose our desires
and control our freedom?

Or would it be
'Yes',
yes to hopes and dreams
and life,

an affirmation for our soul,

a word of courage
for our heart?

'God is the strength of my heart.'
Psalm 73:26

relationship & knowing god

If we think about God and try to touch God with our words, it involves relationship. If our existing relationships are difficult, sometimes it makes a relationship with God easier because of need, sometimes harder because of experience. Knowing God is as much about noticing the questions as finding the answers. What are your questions?

The inside of your soul

The inside of your soul is a sacred place,
the essence of your being.
I can see its contours in your face
but cannot come within.
You hold the key.
The inside of your soul is a secret place
where only spirit dwells.
Welcome God in,
an unseen partnership of grace.
Your soul need not be alone,
it can be God's home.

'We can never lose God because God is twinned eternally to the soul. Once we awaken to the beauty which is God there is a great sense of homecoming.'

John O'Donohue, *Divine Beauty*

Feng shui

Silly
to order my rooms
aright

and not order my soul
to have room
for God!

'I learned the great truth that a friendship with a see-through being required the same sacrifices as a friendship with an opaque one i.e. attention and time.'
Lionel Blue, *Hitchhiking to Heaven*

The right road

My way into the future starts tomorrow
from where I am today.
If I missed the best road yesterday
(or all the years before)
I haven't left God waiting
at that ending.

God is here now.
I can find my way any day I recognise
I've been walking the wrong road
alone
and want to walk
the right road together.

**Does your life feel like the wrong road
or the right road?**

relationship

A relationship with God

A relationship with God is like bread.
You need it every day and if you
leave it, it goes stale.

A relationship with God is like tinned soup.
It's always there, ready to open,
warm up and nourish.

Are you a soup or a bread merchant?

Family forever

I have a daughter who grew in my body
and I nursed as a baby; she looks like me.
I have another I didn't know until four
years old; she looks different.
I love both my daughters more
than I could ever have imagined.
They are mine completely, for ever.
They are my family.

God has children who have always
belonged. They know God's ways and
the Spirit shines in their faces. There are
others who started off on their own
not knowing or wanting God,
their faces not facing heaven.

But with God we can be adopted at any
age with any face. And then we are
completely God's.
We are family forever.

In some ways we have always been part of God's family.
In some ways we need to join up.

relationship

Surprise

God sometimes comes like this
on quiet feet
like spring slipping slowly
under winter's door
so you don't notice
the growing light
until the air surprises you
with welcome warmth.

God is often quieter than we would expect.

relationship

Nearer to me

God,
not just there
but here,
not just then but now,
not other
but mine, not dead
but alive.

God,
nearer to me
than my thoughts,
stronger in me
than my blood,
more patient with me
than myself,
more lover of me
than my heart.

When I think about a relationship with God it always slides into intimacy.

relationship

Welcome

To see God as father or friend is not an
excuse
to reduce God to a man-sized mentor,
tame and safe.

They are words that represent my
welcome
into the wild wonder
of God's flowing mystery.

Yea !!!

Religion

There are many beliefs, structures,
practices in religion
which kept me away from God.
Some may have been right for a previous season
or may be right now for a different person.

But I need not be put off by religion,
it does not dictate my spirituality.
It is a resource for me.
I can learn from faith stories,
find roots and continuity,
service and community,
fellow travellers on the journey.

Is religion a help or a hindrance for you?

Imagination

Imagination
isn't the opposite of truth
or limited to fairy-tales.

It is the artist
of my inner world
without which
I cannot dream dreams
or hold aims.

It is the seed of hope
and the fuel of faith.

Without imagination
I cannot know God.

Imagination expands our knowing.

Understand

Sometimes
I stumble on
something of God
I do not understand
and turn away

as if I had
expected
that I could
understand
everything.

Has anything made you turn away?

Apprehend God

It isn't just religious sources that help me
apprehend God.
I can turn to any science or art and let
the patterns and beauty of the universe
increase my awe.

**'All of life, every scrap and morsel,
is sacred, creative, and charged
with meaning.'**
Julia Cameron, *God Is No Laughing Matter*

Sky

I can go a whole day without noticing
the sky
although it's huge and always there

like God.

'At the heart of all creation, at the birth of every creature, at the centre of each moment is your splendour.'

J. Philip Newell,
Sounds of the Eternal: A Celtic Psalter

Letting go

If God is to be truly God to me
I can't just seek God in light and joy,
turning my back on darkness and pain
and walling them out with fear.

Where would I find God
(or know my own depths)
when the wall crashes
or silence seeps through the cracks?

God is in inbreath and outbreath,
in movement and stillness,
in shining and in suffering,
pulsing in words of beauty
and being beyond and beneath all language.

God is to be found in living
and in letting go.

Letting go even of God,
of our image of God and our trying to connect.
Letting go to allow me, and God,
to just be.

'The highest and loftiest thing that one can let go of is to let go of God for the sake of God.'
Meister Eckhart

God's box

When
the box that I've built
to define the things of God
breaks
it feels like
I've lost God.

But I haven't lost God.

Just the box.

This feels scary when it happens, yet it's good – I end up with a bigger view of God.

A follower of God

To be a follower of God isn't to exchange a life
of sin for a life of safety.

It is to know the fire that birthed
the universe, to be transformed from
an image breaker to an image maker,
co-creating with God.

It isn't to celebrate history and ritual
but to dance so hard with a celebration of life
that it stamps upon injustice
and calls out the celebrant in others.

To be a follower of God
is not to build walls around a belief group
but to be part of the community of creation.

It isn't to expect beds of roses without thorns
but to know that beds of thorns will have roses.

It is a prophetic call to see and hear, to
respond with compassion and not fear anger.

It is to change the world by changing my life.

It is to be the face of God in my time.

My manifesto!
What would you write for your manifesto?

love & jesus

Have you experienced
God's love?
What is your response when
you see the name 'Jesus'?

God's love

I used to think God's love
was like light from the sun
reaching everything and everyone
automatically

but that's not how love works.

Love can't be automatic,
love means caring and choosing,
relating and knowing,
giving.
Love is personal.

God's love is love I can know
and bigger than I can imagine.

It holds acceptance and challenge,
intimacy and space,
security and surprise.

God's love isn't just love,
it is part of the presence of
God.

All love bears the imprint of God's love.

The emotions of God?

What are the emotions
of God? What are the tides within
the navy night of soul that carries
God's name? Do they feed
each other, joy playing banjo
on sorrow's strings while love holds
anger like a crown?
What are the swellings of breast that
charm
the bees upon the blossom, that fire
the voyagers' return?

I have heard it whispered
that night after night
God sits holding tenderness
on soft knees
while murmuring our name.

What are the emotions of God?
After R.S.Thomas

Unwanted

To feel unwanted is like a tree without roots,
needing love but not knowing how to trust it.
It is worse in some lands.
If born outside marriage I would have
no status, position or name.

What a wonder
that God can be father/mother/friend to me,
a love to understand and nourish my soul,
a pure well that my roots can tap, drink
and dig deep.

Inside my soul-space I can find an echo,
the sound of my name whispered
to the rhythm of God's love,
the beat of eternity in my heart.

'God said "Can a mother forget the baby at her breast and have no compassion on the child she has born? Though she may forget, I will not forget you! See, I have engraved you on the palms of my hands".'
Isaiah 49:15–16

love

You are my sun

You are my sun
though on a winter's day
you're far away.

You are my sun
though at night
I can't see you.

You are my sun
though the clouds
often hide you.

You are my sun
and today
I can feel you.

You are my sun
and my life
turns towards you.

What metaphor would you use for God's love in your life?

Absence

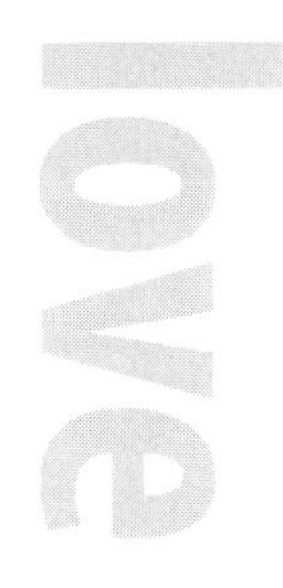

Is it that those who feel no glow,
who see no thread connecting
their frame to your hearth
mistake your presence for absence
as they know no other?
Is it as a plane speeding
steadily through the night air,
eating the miles to China, feels still?

Is it the core of an apple
that cannot burst with taste until bitten,
that cannot fruit with life until planted?
Is it harmonics of the air that only dogs hear,
directions in the wind that only swallows find,
sources of the stream that only salmon mind?

Or is it the quickening space between lovers
who know not to rush and thrust
but hold the pool of heart
like a bubble between stretched fingers
even when far away,

even when far away.

If God's presence was obvious and irresistible, would that be love?

love

Water the wilderness

God's love
isn't a fountain for my garden
but a spring
flowing through me
to water the wilderness.

What changes would love make to your life?

Compassion

The key to compassion
isn't to look to my heart for love
or my neighbour for need
but to look around
and see the web of life
networking us all in
interdependence.

**'The best way to know God is
to love many things.'**
Vincent Van Gogh

jesus

Monopoly

Christians
haven't got a monopoly
on Jesus.

Often our view of Jesus is affected by Christians or the church. Can you see Jesus beyond that?

Finding my own

Different people and religions
see Jesus
in different ways.

It's easy
to disagree with other beliefs
about Jesus

rather than finding my own.

If Jesus is not just a historical figure but represents something of God accessible to us today, how would that help us engage with God?

Lodestone

Jesus is a mark
of God filling and affirming
the natural world,
incarnating the carnal,
blessing the physical by taking on flesh,
destroying the barriers between
material and spiritual,
between sacred and common, between
senses and sensing,
between sanctity and self.

Jesus is my lodestone
for a spirituality which is not emasculated,
a God who is not distant,
a world that is not worthless,
a faith that is part
of life.

Now I know God can be
as intimate as blood,
as real as breath.

Is Jesus important?
This is part of my answer.

Resurrection

I find it no surprise
that death and resurrection
are at the cosmic heart
of God

when I see caterpillars
transform into butterflies,
night into day, seed
split and broken
by the intimate probing
of a shoot,
winter dying its own death
for the first green kiss
of spring
and hearts holding hope
in the midst of grief
with memories of loved ones
that can never die.

**Resurrection is a potent myth.
It is central to the story of Jesus and
its promise – not restoring the old but
transcending it; creating a spiritual
body, the substance of heaven.**

Two commandments

Jesus said
you can hang all spiritual truth
on two commandments.

One is to love our neighbour as
ourselves,
something I remember I ought to do
but often fall short.

Yet the other is more important
and so easily forgotten –
to love God with all that I am
and all that I do.

Which two 'commandments' would you choose as a basis for life?

The news in heaven

The news in heaven isn't like our news. It doesn't major on earthquakes, assassinations and corruption with one small human interest story at the end if there is time.

The news in heaven trumpets the joy of a baby, the warmth of a friend, the green of spring. It notices the faithfulness of those who are always there, not just the chaos caused by someone who isn't.

The news in heaven doesn't shout our faults and selfishness but declares with them our saying sorry, our best intentions, our putting things right. But all secret evil, abuse hidden in respectable homes and governments, would be noted in heaven.

The news in heaven doesn't just announce winners but appreciates participants, it doesn't follow celebrity fashions but finds good in people's hearts. The news in heaven notices a sparrow that has died and the hairs on our head.

Even an earthquake wouldn't look the same, for a focus of disaster is a focus for prayer. Covering the fractured earth and lives and hopes is a mountain of caring that tells stories of pain and love in heaven.

The news in heaven isn't like our news because the lead story isn't our pain or success but God's, the journey of Jesus, the conversion of death, the remodelling of heaven to be our home.

How does Jesus link us with heaven?

God's face

Jesus
is the human face
of God.

Can you imagine God's face?
Can you imagine Jesus' face?

wisdom & wonder

Wisdom and wonder are
gifts of God.
Do you look for wisdom?
What makes your heart shine
with wonder?

The infinite

My need for the infinite
fuels my dreams
and my destiny.

Yet so often I sell myself short
and crowd out my longing for God
with the pursuit of pleasure
or possessions.

Without God there is no destiny.

The invisible

I can act
as if the world I inhabit
is the physical one
I can see and predict,

living life
on the surface

instead of owning
the world
of the invisible –

thoughts, feelings, beliefs,
my origins
and my destiny,
spirit and energy,

a fluid ocean
within and without,
my interface with God

'There is not in the Celtic way of seeing a great gap between heaven and earth. Rather, the two are seen as inseparably intertwined.'

J. Philip Newell, *Listening for the Heartbeat of God*

Be real

The important thing with God
is not to be religious
but to be real.

'Religion often suffers from a great amnesia; it constantly insists on the seriousness of God and forgets the magic of the Divine Glory.'
John O'Donohue, *Eternal Echoes*

Respect

It doesn't honour God
to revere the religious symbols we have made
and not respect the creation
God has made:

the world, nature,
each other.

Creation can be seen as the primary sacrament.

Going with the flow

There is the strength of steel,
stiffly resisting all movement and pressure
as waves crash and tides retreat.

Or there is the strength of seaweed,
the holdfast secure on the rock,
flowing and weaving with the waves,
accommodating all movement and
pressure,
a living harmony.

Sometimes we are strongest when we don't feel strong at all.

Feelings

Feelings, imagination,
bodies
are as important to God as
thought, will,
conscience.

'The most beautiful and profound emotion we can experience is the sensation of the mystical.'
Albert Einstein

Laughter

Because God is important we can think that means serious. Because God is bigger and better than us and we screw up we can think that means serious with us.

We forget that if you are the biggest and best you don't have to be serious. If you know how stuff works you can relax and have fun.

Was God serious when planning the turkey or the baboon's bottom? Did we think *we* invented laughter?

Next time we laugh so much that every cell tingles,
know it is a sacrament and give God a smile.

Traditional views of holiness often shun laughter. Do you agree?

Peacemaker

One of the greatest things to be is a peacemaker.

Wherever I walk, in high places or at home, I can be God's ambassador of peace.

Being a peacemaker brings God into a situation without even mentioning God's name.

Everywhere

God is not
just there in prayer

does not just relate
to religion

but imbues all of life
with presence.

If you could colour God's presence, what colours would you use?

wonder

Mystery

Scientists and theologians have a lot
in common.
They see, they question, they explain.
Theories and theologies, boxes in which to fit
reality,
seen and unseen,
a comfortable, controllable world.
But if there is no mystery
it doesn't feed the heart.

Mystery is as much part of the universe, and
God, as fact –
breath and bones, shadow and substance,
secret and revealed.

To know someone well is also to know
their difference from me,
to respect their secret places.
It's the same with God, and with our planet.
Approach both with awe and wonder as well as
science or certainty.

For some things candlelight is better than
spotlight
and not knowing is better than understanding
all.

How can you tap into the wonder of mystery?

Light is a wave

Light is a wave and light is a particle. Life is a journey towards God and a being in God. Following God is finding self and is dying to self. My choice is a freedom to act and is part of God's plan.

It's such a freedom to hold contrasting realities together without needing to reconcile them.

wonder

Is it an accident?

Is it an accident
that plants produce oxygen
and need carbon dioxide,
while CO2 is our waste
and we need oxygen to live?

Did it just happen so,
a chance coupling that allowed
the profusion of life
on this planet?

Was there an intelligence
inside green cells
that programmed their efforts
to ensure our survival?

Or is there an intelligence
bigger than both of us
who planned it all?

Faith and science can interact creatively.

Wonder

An oak tree grows
from a small seed
to a huge tree
built from earth and
air, water
and sunshine.

And I can grow flowers
and fruits,
lawns and corn,
bushes and berries,
food for living and feasting.

All I need is a seed with
God's blueprint
hidden inside,
plant it and water and
let it grow rich
on air
and on sunshine

'Keep a green tree in your heart and perhaps the singing bird will come.'
Chinese proverb

Opportunities

How awful if all my plans worked out exactly
and there was no room for surprise.

How common to wake each morning
with my mind and my day set

instead of expecting and
welcoming changes,
openings for new encounters,

opportunities for patience
or for adventure.

Try seeing challenges as adventures.

trust & darkness

Trust and doubt can exist at the same time and can hone each other. What do you believe? What do you doubt? What different ways do you deal with darkness?

Trusting

I passed
this small fall before
and now here I am again
in the darkening night,
the stream still flowing and talking,
still breaking and bubbling white
and will be all through the night
though none sees or hears,
the rock cradling the brown waters
as they hang smooth as beer
then fall laughing and frothing
over its bony arm.

In another place
the dark is hiding
the soft contours of my children's faces
blown by sleep,
breathing the seconds of the night
as they pool in dreams
then rush sparkling away.
And I must trust
this flow will not fail
though I do not watch or wait,
held by arms I cannot see,
carrying secret memories.

Love means learning to trust.

trust

Faith

I show my faith in God
when I'm angry but I don't shout,
or when grey blankets the sky
and I remember the sun.

I show my faith in God
when I'm depressed but I hold hope
or when you hurt me and I forgive.

My faith in God is the rock behind me
when my back's against the wall.
My faith in God fills my empty pocket
when I've used the last of my resources.

My faith isn't a Sunday bonnet
but is blood and muscle.
My faith can live in dreams, in dustbins.

Faith is like
a coloured filter in my mind,
a special perfume in the air.
Faith in God is like faith in life.

**Faith in God also means trusting God
in myself and in others.**

Believing in God

Believing in God is not
wearing rose-tinted glasses;
an easy option;
a certainty to silence questions;
a way of avoiding pain.

Believing in God is
recognising horror and choosing to forgive;
facing the music and choosing to dance;
feeling hurt and choosing to love;
being uncertain and choosing to trust;
knowing the downside and choosing life.

Believing in God changes me first.

trust

Belief

To believe
isn't to adopt a rigid architecture
of mind and soul.

Belief is a warm current
that feeds my life and others'
and is fed itself
by the waters that it meets,

mingling, changing,
growing.

'Some may find their journey has taken them to places they never expected; there are those who have found faith in deeper or diverse ways, and others who have suffered the pain of losing faith. Yet remember this is a moment on the journey, our story is not yet finished.'

Gary Collins, *Sacred Space Ritual*

Trust

Trust
is an opening door
in my heart

that doesn't guard
its own
too fiercely

but trusts that giving
will not lead to loss
but to receiving

trust

**Being generous is having a 'good eye'
that lights the whole body.**

See Matthew 6:22

trust

Rules

It is a mistake to trust the rules that we make
about God
more than the Spirit God gives us.

Rules restrict but the Spirit brings life.

Sometimes

Sometimes
the shout of my heart
is so loud I can't hear you,
sometimes
the blackness around
hides your face.
Sometimes
the pain is so great
I can't feel you
or understand
the route my path takes.
Sometimes
life isn't right
and I can't bear
the wait.

But telling you this
is my faith.

'It is at least possible that hard times come upon us not as punishments but as stringent blessings. Spiritual and creative breakthroughs are the frequent fruit of time in the desert, a sudden vivid flowering as when the desert floor comes vibrantly alive after a rare and sudden rain. Droughts can be survived. Desert time can be turned to good purpose if we are willing to listen and endure.'

Julia Cameron, *God Is No Laughing Matter*

Don't pretend

I can be real with God,
I don't have to hide my depression and fears.

I don't have to pretend with God,
when grief strikes
I don't have to smile and sing,
God understands tears.

It's OK to be angry when life hurts,
God doesn't need protecting
from how I feel.

Even hatred or despair aren't too low
to let God in.
God shares my heart
and can listen to its pain.

We can't shock God.

For give

If you hurt me and couldn't help it
I may excuse you.

If you hurt me and there is no excuse
I can forgive you.

If I don't I will be holding on
to the evil done to me.
If I didn't like it, why hold on to it?
Why rehearse it for it only multiplies it?

Why afford it room in my heart
for it will only twist it?

Why stay the victim when I can be free?

Forgiveness is the morning-after pill
to prevent unwanted hurt.

**Some think forgiveness is weak.
But there is a great strength in being
able to overcome anger, bitterness,
hurt or disappointment.**

Different whispers

There are different whispers in my ear,
in my belly, in my blood.
The voice of self that feeds my needs and my desires,
a necessary urgency that can grow
fat and self-indulgent.
Echoes from the past
that mould my present
with sticky fingers of security or of fears.
And sometimes dark desires erupt
that would twist fortune and tarnish
my destiny.

But silently wooing
in the brightest and blackest seasons
is a voice of love, unsettling selfishness,
calming fears and offering a true direction.

The spirit of God isn't imprisoned in heaven,
doesn't live in church or temple,
isn't just present when I pray.

The wild goose who stirs longings for
adventures of spirit
cannot control or be controlled.
That cry is the echo of my heart.

Love has a dramatic effect on inner discord.

The geography of evil

I don't understand the geography of evil,
I don't often know why,

can't pin God's hand to the cause of
my sorrows,

can't make God take the blame for
my life.

But I can find God within disaster
salvaging hope, promising life.

darkness

God is blamed when a disaster happens but rarely thanked when something wonderful happens.

Fear is

Fear is a dark cave
but I can give you a candle.

Fear is not knowing where you are
but I can show you the road.

Fear is believing your worst dreams
but I can give you hope.

Fear is being small when the problem is big
but I can show you God.

Although darkness seems stronger than light, when they meet, light wins!

Guilt

Guilt kills; its black tentacles freeze the soul.
Convincing myself I'm blameless only hides
it deeper.

Sometimes it's worse if I know of
God's goodness,
if I think I'll always fall short of
God's measure
so stay away.

But God's love is as vast and creative and
active as God.
It's not put off by my wickedness,
or pettiness, or grudging goodness.

It measured my shortfall and sent Jesus
to make up what was lacking and more
it opened the door.

So if I call on God with a heart weighed
with guilt
I can step into a stream of forgiveness
that will wash away the blame forever.

It doesn't help to bury guilt, to pretend we were not at fault, to blame others. Admitting it and asking forgiveness is a wonderful way to be free and not as scary as it sounds.

Haiku for healing

The breath of winter,
alone with dark dreams, disease
eats bitter thoughts.

The touch of summer,
joy is a warm wind, with
laughter healing comes.

Joy is one of the best medicines.

Coiled springs

It is easy to take offence
letting little things (or big)
slide in under my skin
and lodge there in unquiet memory,
disturbing my peace.

It is easy to walk through life
tight with these forgotten emotions
tarnishing the world that I see.

It is possible
to stop and notice the coiled springs within
and to ease them into opening
with deep breaths of kindness and
forgiveness.

'The greatest reassurance and safety that can be given to your body is the warm attention of your own mind.'
William Bloom, *The Endorphin Effect*

Stress

It's hard to change the habit of stressing
when fear is so seductive,
my role and result seem so important
and failure is my default setting.

My body becomes a temple of adrenalin and
controlled panic and it is hard for tight
muscles and mind
to relax and respond to any faith I find.
Easier to start off with trust as my inner
smile.

But if caught up in tension, as well as hot
baths, deep breaths and self-kindness
I try noticing,
noticing the pattern of fern-fronds or oak
leaves,
the sparkle of spiders' nets, the support of
ground,

seeing the texture and weave of cloth,
the interplay of colours,
the presence of air, the shapes that
surround,

so letting wonderment grow out of dark soil
and perspective light my tunnel of
frustration.

**Stress comes from reacting to a situation
not the situation itself.**

prayer & blessings

Do you find it easy to pray?
Do you pray with words or
pictures or objects, with
silence, music or movement,
with a verse or saying,
or do you pray impromptu?
Experiment, there isn't one
right way.
Prayer and blessings – what
are your blessings?

Sacred

Confining prayer
to a set time or place or words
limits my relationship
with God.

Prayer is breathing
worries and wonders to God
as they touch me,
an ebb and flow of life as it is lived
making everything sacred
and dynamic.

'I eventually did manage to tell God in prayer my very mixed motives. He calmed me down and told me that I should leave the worrying to him. I had never before realised how helpful it was to have a God. I blessed him.'

Lionel Blue, *Hitchhiking to Heaven*

prayer

Gratitude

The thing I say
most often to God
isn't 'please'
or 'help'
but
'thank you'.

Not a formal prayer,
just appreciation
marking the moments
of my day.

Can you tell if someone has been drinking?
Can you tell if someone has been smoking?
Can you tell if someone has been praying?

Speaking to God

Speaking to God
without learning the
language of love

is like speaking French
with an English accent.

'Lovers say, "Talk to me." We speak in many spiritual traditions of God as the beloved, and yet when we think of talking to God we find ourselves freezing into the formality of prayer. Lovers use their own words to speak their heart, yet often when we pray we reach for a "great prayer". Like the lover who sends a Shakespeare sonnet, we often address God as through a filter, or, perhaps better, an interpreter. Maybe it's time we spoke to God more candidly.'

Julia Cameron, *God Is No Laughing Matter.*

prayer

Prayer

I breathe out
you hear me,
I breathe in
you see me.
I reach out
you hold me,
I sit still
you wait in me.
My blood beats
your dreams in me.
I can't lose
your beat in me.
You hold back
I'm thirsty,
you pour in
I give away.
I'm thinking
your wishes,
you're wanting
to answer.

'In the silence of our prayer we should be able to sense the roguish smile of a joyful God who, despite all the chaos and imperfection, ultimately shelters everything.'
John O'Donohue, *Eternal Echoes*

The answer

Sometimes I can try too hard,
bearing down with prayer and urgency
on my desired future,
my mind as hard as my resolve

instead of letting God's peace fill me first
and listening to the soft lapping of God's
possibilities
against my desires
until the two are one voice that beats in
my blood
and summons the answer
to my needs.

'Prayer is taking silent time to overhear your soul's conversation with God.'
John O'Donohue

Busyness

I am separated from God
not by 'sin'
but by busyness,

by not recognising God
in the moments of my day,

by not living life
as a prayer.

Living life as a prayer isn't shutting down on living so that we can focus on God. It is living life in its fullness, aware of God and ourselves and our world.

Me

I don't have to do
anything special
for God to be interested in me.

I don't have to be
clever, or good, or religious.

In fact, I think God sometimes
prefers people who aren't,
people who know they
aren't perfect
and don't pretend.

God is interested in me
just because I'm me.

And when I find it hard to believe,
I can offer up my desire to believe
as a prayer.

'Prayer is never wasted. It always brings transformation. Through prayer we learn to see with the eyes of the soul.'
John O'Donohue, *Eternal Echoes*

prayer

Give me a boat to ride the seasons

Give me a boat to ride the seasons
so I don't stumble
when summer falls to Fall.

May I ride through the silver spray
of shorter days
and not fear cold nights.

And when crunchy leaves and lanterns
have given way to the
bleak wasting of the year
may I float on your hidden sun

to be brought once more to the
quickening boughs, the shock of yellow
and the greening of the trees.

Then I may alight and wander through
summer fields of gold,
a coming home.

What would you pray for?

Today

Welcome to the gift of today.
This is a day unlike all others and when gone
it cannot be retrieved.
This is a day when I can hold the interface
between change and routine.
This is a day breathed by God who shines
in all its possibilities. This is a new day.

This is a day to leave behind the regrets of yesterday
and start again, fresh and absorbed by hope.
This is a day for me to make my own.
Today I can choose to not just see the grey,
to not let busyness cram every corner
or boredom kill my creativity.
Today I can notice all the blessings that lap at my shore,
or look for opportunities to quietly bless others.

I can count the smiles, see the ever-changing shapes
between leaf and tree, between earth and sky
and as I see them, they are mine and can enlarge
my soul.
And even if today holds great pain
or the death of those most precious,
there are gentle hands to hold me
and carry me through to tomorrow.

'Recognise the huge, concealed potential of a day for soul-making.'
John O'Donohue, *Eternal Echoes*

blessings

A birthday song

Life comes round again
full of light,
a vessel to carry me forward
into my next year,
into any night that
might lurk or try to steal
this,
the joy of taste,
the universe inside, wide
with captured colour and
budding thought,
the songbird's charm,
the soft hair that grows
on the skin of friendship
to keep it warm.

Two of my favourite blessings –
birthdays and friends.
What are your favourite blessings?

Five minutes of heaven

There is an alley that I walk down each day
to take my girls to school.
It is framed with green
as branches hang in archways overhead
and may flowers and cow parsley
glow white amongst the new leaves.

Some days I don't see them
as busy thoughts claim total attention,
or else I look down and only see
rotting leaves, dog dirt and litter.

Each day I can choose
to walk in the busyness or dirt of the
world,
or look up and breathe in
five minutes of heaven.

'Christ was a carpenter. He walked barefoot and heard the angels singing. Go for a walk in your most comfortable shoes. Walk slowly and listen to what the angels say.'
Julia Cameron, *God Is No Laughing Matter*

If I had stayed at home

If I had stayed at home on this cold-curling morn
I wouldn't have seen the frost hang curtains of still leaves
or coat the house tops with sugar.

I wouldn't have been part of the chemistry that brings invisibility to light, stealing vapour from the air
to crunch in crystals on silver lawns,
I wouldn't have witnessed the sun and air
conspire to win it back again in warm breaths.

If I had stayed warm at home I wouldn't have seen
the sailing moon silvering the blue-wash sky
or gulls float on the thinner air.

If I hadn't been abroad in the breaking of first light
I wouldn't have seen the seasons of trees at this cusp of the year
when summer and autumn colours linger
among the branches of black.

I wouldn't have felt the turning earth
as sunstrips move shadows and ice,
I wouldn't have felt living air on my face
or heavy ground under my feet,
I wouldn't have felt this day
if I had stayed at home.

We can miss blessings by staying comfortable.

Umbria

Thanks and oh yes
for this bright-folding day
green-girdled and sun-stretched
heavy with lazy stillness,
stirred but not shaken by
the pigeon's coos,
the lizards' scatter,
the breeze's whisper.
Children and friends still in bed,
figs ripening and falling
overhead,
warm mountains, patchwork fields
and hill villages fill the view
and nothing to be done
save what we want to do.

The blessing of holidays. If you can't go away, find space in your usual routine to do something different that will bless you.

A blessing

May God be a home to you, an anchor
and a safe place.
May God be the wind to you, carrying
you into a new day.

May God be your settling down and your
rising up,
your certainty of security and your agent
of change.

May God be the moon of night and the
sun of day to you.
May God be what is now and what is to
come to you.

May God be music and silence to you.
May God be to you.

What would you like God to be to you?

When you see trees

When you see trees,
think of God.

When love throws you a line
or friends warm your heart,
think of God.

When you are lonely or in pain,
think of God.

When your day is blessed
by sunshine
or insight,
forgiveness or laughter,
think of God.

Can blessing be found in any situation?

God is here

The tide is out now.
The sun is setting on
gleaming sand,
seagulls wheel in the
full air
and a white shell lies
in the ripples at my feet.

Suddenly love like a blanket
wraps itself round
my heart
and sings.

God is here.

God is here.

Acknowledgements

The author and publishers would like to thank the following for permission to include copyright material.

p. 105, William Bloom, *The Endorphin Effect,* Piatkus, 2001.

pp. 37 & 94, Gary Collins, *Sacred Space Ritual: A Harvest of Our Selves,* October 2005. gary@absence-presence.co.uk

pp. 42 & 109, Lionel Blue, *Hitchhiking to Heaven,* Hodder & Stoughton, 2005.

pp. 52, 97, 111 & 119, Julia Cameron, *God Is No Laughing Matter: Observations and Objections on the Spiritual Path,* Pan Books, 2001.

p. 76, J. Philip Newell, *Listening for the Heartbeat of God: A Celtic Spirituality,* SPCK, 1997.

pp. 24 & 53, J. Philip Newell, *Sounds of the Eternal: A Celtic Psalter,* Canterbury Press, 2002, © Canterbury Press, an imprint of Hymns Ancient & Modern Ltd. Used by permission.

p. 19, John O'Donohue, *Anam Cara: Spiritual Wisdom from the Celtic World,* Bantam Books, 1999.

pp. 32 & 41, John O'Donohue, *Divine Beauty: The Invisible Embrace,* Bantam Books, 2004.

pp. 77, 112, 115 & 117, John O'Donohue, *Eternal Echoes: Exploring Our Hunger to Belong,* Bantam Books, 2000.

pp. 38 & 61, Scripture quotations taken from the HOLY BIBLE, NEW INTERNATIONAL VERSION.
Copyright © 1973, 1978, 1984 by International Bible Society.
Used by permission of Hodder & Stoughton Publishers, A member of the Hachette Livre UK Group.
All rights reserved.
"NIV" is a registered trademark of International Bible Society.
UK trademark number 1448790.

Every effort has been made to contact copyright holders The publishers apologise to anyone whose rights have been inadvertently overlooked, and will be happy to rectify any errors or omissions.

Bibliography

William Bloom, *The Endorphin Effect*, Piatkus, 2001.

Lionel Blue, *Hitchhiking to Heaven,* Hodder & Stoughton, 2005.

Julia Cameron, *The Artist's Way: A Course in Discovering and Recovering your Creative Self,* Pan Books, 1997.

Julia Cameron, *God Is No Laughing Matter: Observations and Objections on the Spiritual Path,* Pan Books, 2001.

Gary Collins, *Sacred Space Ritual: A Harvest of Our Selves,* October 2005.

Matthew Fox, *Meditations with Meister Eckhart,* Bear & Co., 1987.

J. Philip Newell, *Listening for the Heartbeat of God: A Celtic Spirituality,* SPCK, 1997.

J. Philip Newell, *Sounds of the Eternal: A Celtic Psalter,* Canterbury Press, 2002.

John O'Donohue, *Anam Cara: Spiritual Wisdom from the Celtic World,* Bantam Books, 1997.

John O'Donohue, *Divine Beauty: The Invisible Embrace,* Bantam Books, 2003.

John O'Donohue, *Eternal Echoes: Exploring our Hunger to Belong,* Bantam Books, 1998.

Mary Oliver, *Thirst,* Beacon Press, 2006, Bloodaxe Books, 2007.

Tess Ward, *The Celtic Wheel of the Year: Celtic and Christian Seasonal Prayers,* O Books, 2007.

Index

beginnings & endings
Inner wellies 9
In the beginning 10
Spirit beings 11
I have seen a miracle 12
Glimpsing God 13
Cross roads 14
For Peggy 15
Heaven 16
Autumn leaf 17
For Sammy 18
When I am about to die 19
At the end of the day 20

humanness & godness
Three needs 23
Only one 24
Heart 25
Beauty 26
Source of strength 27
Blob days 28
Permission 29
Community 30
God 31
God participates 32
I need a God who can suffer 33
Heartbeat 34
God changes 35
God's name 36
Outside 37
Yes 38

relationship & knowing god
The inside of your soul 41
Feng shui 42
The right road 43
A relationship with God 44
Family forever 45
Surprise 46
Nearer to me 47
Welcome 48
Religion 49
Imagination 50
Understand 51
Apprehend God 52
Sky 53
Letting go 54
God's box 55
A follower of God 56

love & jesus
God's love 59
The emotions of God 60
Unwanted 61
You are my sun 62
Absence 63
Water the wilderness 64
Compassion 65
Monopoly 66
Finding my own 67
Lodestone 68
Resurrection 69
Two commandments 70
The news in heaven 71
God's face 72

wisdom & wonder
The infinite 75
The invisible 76
Be real 77
Respect 78
Going with the flow 79
Feelings 80
Laughter 81
Peacemaker 82
Everywhere 83
Mystery 84
Light is a wave 85
Is it an accident? 86
Wonder 87
Opportunities 88

trust & darkness
Trusting 91
Faith 92
Believing in God 93
Belief 94
Trust 95
Rules 96
Sometimes 97
Don't pretend 98
For give 99
Different whispers 100
The geography of evil 101
Fear is 102
Guilt 103
Haiku for healing 104
Coiled springs 105
Stress 106

prayer & blessings
Sacred 109
Gratitude 110
Speaking to God 111
Prayer 112
The answer 113
Busyness 114
Me 115
Give me a boat to ride the seasons 116
Today 117
A birthday song 118
Five minutes of heaven 119
If I had stayed at home 120
Umbria 121
A blessing 122
When you see trees 123
God is here 124